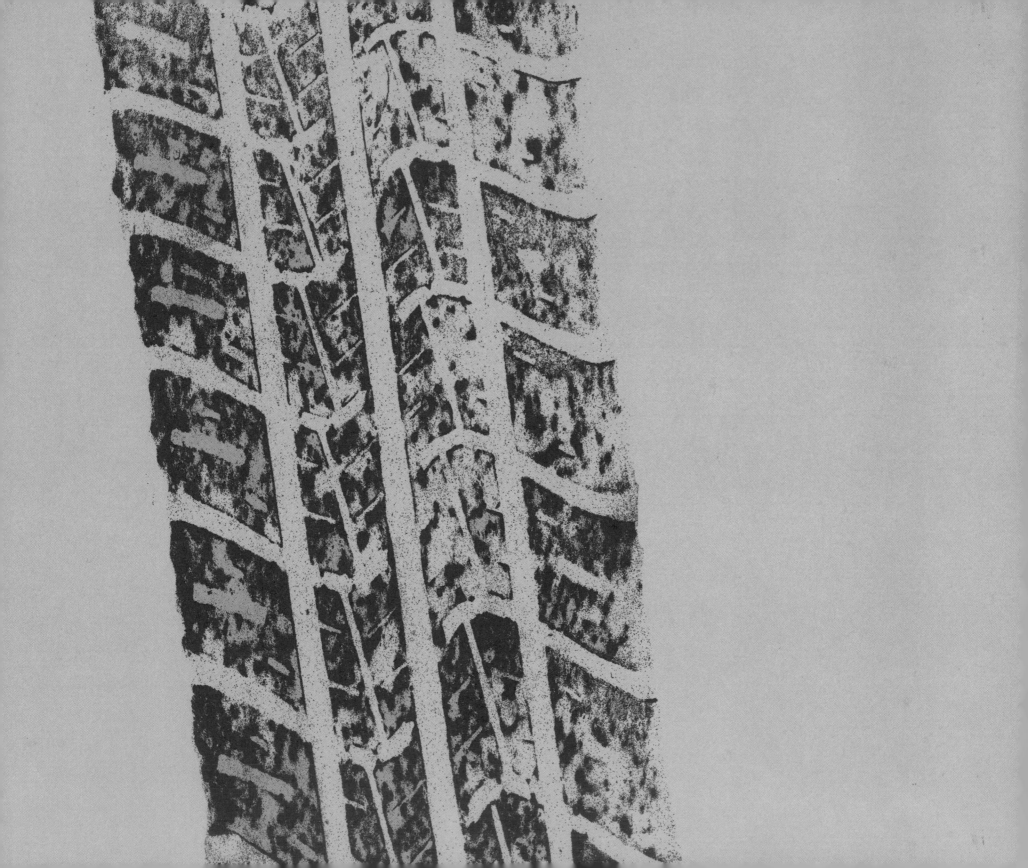

I DRIVE A TRACTOR

by **Sarah Bridges**

illustrated by **Amy Bailey Muehlenhardt**

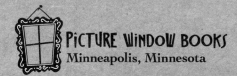

PICTURE WINDOW BOOKS

Minneapolis, Minnesota

Thanks to Bill Barnes of the City of Minneapolis
for all of the great stories. S.B.

Editor: Jill Kalz
Designer: Jaime Martens
Page Production: Tracy Kaehler,
Brandie Shoemaker, Zachary Trover
Creative Director: Keith Griffin
Editorial Director: Carol Jones
The illustrations in this book were created digitally.

Picture Window Books
5115 Excelsior Boulevard
Suite 232
Minneapolis, MN 55416
877-845-8392
www.picturewindowbooks.com

Library of Congress Cataloging-in-Publication Data
Bridges, Sarah.
I drive a tractor / by Sarah Bridges ; illustrated by Amy Bailey
Muehlenhardt.
p. cm. — (Working wheels)
Includes bibliographical references and index.
ISBN 1-4048-1609-7 (hardcover)
1. Tractors—Juvenile literature. 2. Tractor driving—Juvenile
literature. I. Title. II. Series.
TL233.15.B77 2006
629.225'2—dc22   2005023146

Thanks to our advisers for their expertise, research, and advice:

Christopher Murray, Marketing Coordinator
Waterloo (Iowa) Implement, Inc.

Susan Kesselring, M.A., Literacy Educator
Rosemount—Apple Valley—Eagan (Minnesota) School District

3

My name is Dylan. I drive a tractor.
My tractor can do all kinds of jobs.
With different attachments, it can
plow fields and cut grass. It can
lift hay bales and scoop dirt.

Tractors come in many different sizes.
Some are as small as a riding lawn
mower. Others have tires that are
taller than a full-grown person.

Each morning, I check my tractor's fluids, engine, joints, and tires. Today, my job is to haul dirt and rocks out of a field. I hook a dump trailer to the back of my tractor.

A tractor driver needs to be careful not to overload his or her tractor. If a load is too heavy, it may damage the tractor's engine.

I climb a small ladder to get to the cab. The cab has glass on all four sides. I can see everything around me.

Newer tractors have heating, air-conditioning, and radios. These things help make drivers more comfortable.

I drive my tractor from the machine shed to the field. A rotating beacon makes it easy for other drivers to see me. I also have an orange triangle on the back of my tractor and trailer. These triangles are called slow-moving vehicle signs.

An orange slow-moving vehicle sign tells drivers that a vehicle goes slower than the speed limit.

I can see cars behind me
in the tractor's side mirrors.
I move to the edge of the road
to let faster vehicles pass.

Most tractors cannot travel faster than 25 miles (40 kilometers) per hour. Because they move so slowly, tractors are usually driven on the shoulder of the road.

Tractor attachments, such as blades and buckets (scoops), can be very heavy. They may weigh 5,000 pounds (2,250 kilograms) or more.

When I get to the field, a loader is already there. It scoops dirt and rocks, lifts the load into the air, and drops it in my trailer.

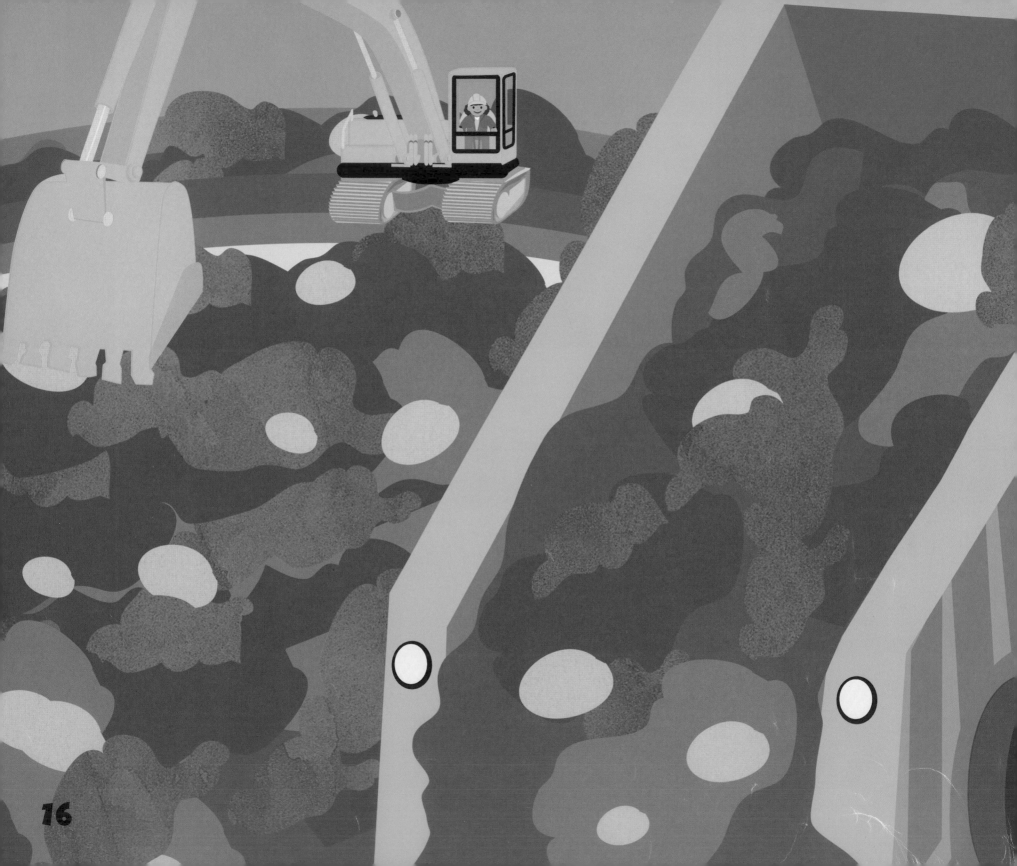

16

When the trailer is full, I drive my tractor to a dump site. I move a lever. The front end of the trailer lifts up, and the load tumbles out the back end.

Dump trailers are most often used to haul dirt, gravel, and wood.

I drive back to the field for another load. But on the way, my tractor makes a terrible squawk. The sound tells me that I don't have enough grease in the wheel joints. I stop the tractor and squirt some grease on them.

Grease is a black, gooey liquid
that helps parts turn easily.

At the end of the day, I drive my tractor back to the machine shed. I check the vehicle one last time. Finally, I close the shed door and let my tractor rest for the night.

Tractors are usually stored in sheds. But sometimes, drivers leave them outside overnight. That way they're in place for the next day.

TRACTOR DIAGRAM

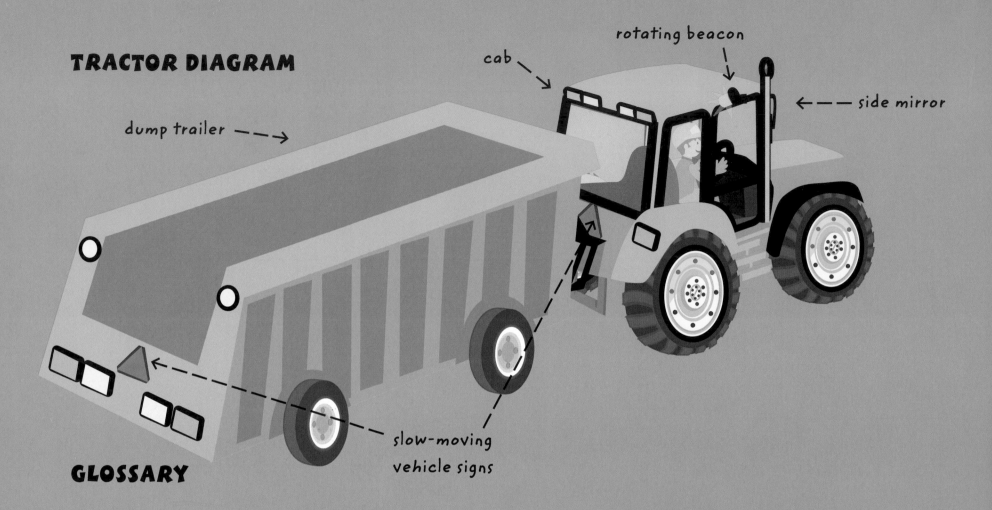

rotating beacon

cab

← − − side mirror

dump trailer − − →

slow-moving
vehicle signs

GLOSSARY

cab—the place in a tractor where the
driver sits

dump trailer—a wagon-like attachment
used for hauling heavy loads

fluids—liquids in the engine that make it
run smoothly

joints—the places where two things
are connected

rotating beacon—a flashing light that warns
other drivers that a vehicle is moving slowly

shoulder—the edge of a road, where vehicles
don't usually drive

FUN FACTS

 Most tractors are "street legal." They have turn signals and other things that make them safe to drive on the road.

 The slow-moving vehicle triangle has special tape along its edges. This tape is reflective, which means that light bounces off it. In the dark, car headlights make the triangle glow.

 Crawler tractors are a special kind of tractor. They move on tracks, just like army tanks. Tracks are metal belts that form a loop around large wheels. The wheels move the tracks. Crawler tractors are used for heavy pulling or pushing. They're also used on steep hills. They're less likely to tip over than wheeled tractors because their tracks grip the ground.

TO LEARN MORE

At the Library

Bingham, Carol. *Tractor.* New York: DK Publishing, 2004.

Rogers, Hal. *Tractors.* Chanhassen, Minn.: Child's World, 2001.

Stickland, Paul. *Tractors.* Columbus, Ohio: Waterbird Books, 2004.

On the Web

FactHound offers a safe, fun way to find Internet sites related to this book. All of the sites on FactHound have been researched by our staff.

1. Visit www.facthound.com

2. Type in this special code for age-appropriate sites: 1404816097

3. Click on the FETCH IT button.

Your trusty FactHound will fetch the best sites for you!

INDEX

LOOK FOR ALL OF THE BOOKS IN THE WORKING WHEELS SERIES:

- I Drive a Backhoe 1-4048-1604-6
- I Drive a Bulldozer 1-4048-0613-X
- I Drive a Crane 1-4048-1605-4
- I Drive a Dump Truck 1-4048-0614-8
- I Drive a Fire Engine 1-4048-1606-2
- I Drive a Freight Train 1-4048-1607-0
- I Drive a Garbage Truck 1-4048-0615-6
- I Drive an Ambulance 1-4048-0618-0
- I Drive a Semitruck 1-4048-0616-4
- I Drive a Snowplow 1-4048-0617-2
- I Drive a Street Sweeper 1-4048-1608-9
- I Drive a Tractor 1-4048-1609-7

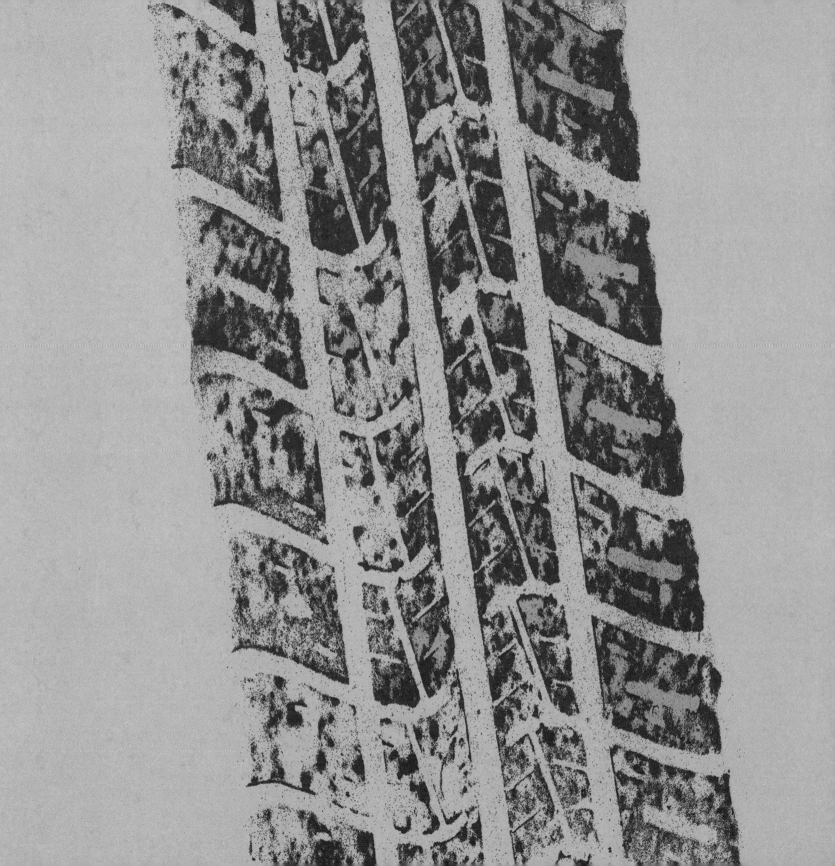